Vocal Selections

SPIRITED

Music from the **Apple Original Film**

Original Songs by Benj Pasek & Justin Paul

ISBN 978-1-70518-765-4

For all works contained herein:
Unauthorized copying, arranging, adapting, recording, internet posting, public performance,
or other distribution of the music in this publication is an infringement of copyright.
Infringers are liable under the law.

Visit Hal Leonard Online at
www.halleonard.com

World headquarters, contact:
Hal Leonard
7777 West Bluemound Road
Milwaukee, WI 53213
Email: info@halleonard.com

In Europe, contact:
Hal Leonard Europe Limited
1 Red Place
London, W1K 6PL
Email: info@halleonardeurope.com

In Australia, contact:
Hal Leonard Australia Pty. Ltd.
4 Lentara Court
Cheltenham, Victoria, 3192 Australia
Email: info@halleonard.com.au

THAT CHRISTMAS MORNING FEELIN'

Music and Lyrics by
BENJ PASEK and JUSTIN PAUL

Copyright © 2022 Pick In A Pinch Music (ASCAP), Breathelike Music (ASCAP) and One Apple Park Songs (ASCAP)
All Rights for Pick In A Pinch Music and Breathelike Music Administered Worldwide by Kobalt Songs Music Publishing
All Rights for One Apple Park Songs Administered by Sony Music Publishing (US) LLC, 424 Church Street, Suite 1200, Nashville, TN 37219
All Rights Reserved   Used by Permission

PAST, PRESENT,
MARLEY &
YET-TO-COME:

This Christ - mas train is par - ty bound! _

MARLEY: *Bring on the Chili of Positive Outcome!* **ALL GHOSTS:**

Building

We're gid - dy with a hol - i - day good -

will gleam _ 'Cause help - in' out is sweet - er than egg - nog cream _

+ PAST:

We might be dead, _ but we're liv - in' that Yule - tide dream! _

PRESENT'S LAMENT

Music and Lyrics by
BENJ PASEK and JUSTIN PAUL

Twinkling Christmas-y wistfulness

Candidly, somewhat freely

Copyright © 2022 Pick In A Pinch Music (ASCAP), Breathelike Music (ASCAP) and One Apple Park Songs (ASCAP)
All Rights for Pick In A Pinch Music and Breathelike Music Administered Worldwide by Kobalt Songs Music Publishing
All Rights for One Apple Park Songs Administered by Sony Music Publishing (US) LLC, 424 Church Street, Suite 1200, Nashville, TN 37219
All Rights Reserved   Used by Permission

Più mosso

to find out if I'm ___ read-y to reach be-yond a Christ-mas morn - ing feel-

- in'? ___ To be hu-man a-gain, a-live ___ once ___ more Take some

swings at the things I missed out on be-fore...

PRESENT: *And there's me in the backyard, goofing around with my two kids who share the same first initial...*

Little Rebecca, and her brother Reggie, or Robert, or... Rawrrrrrr.... I dunno, I'll think of a good R name.

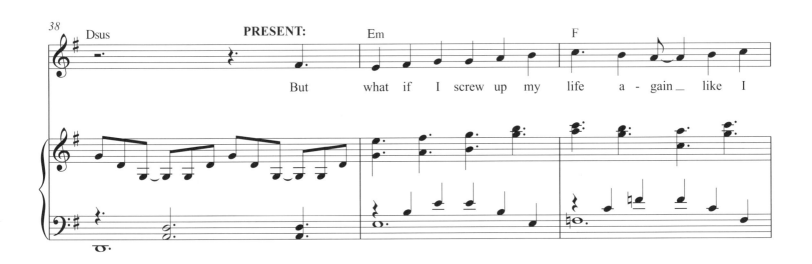

But what if I screw up my life a - gain___ like I

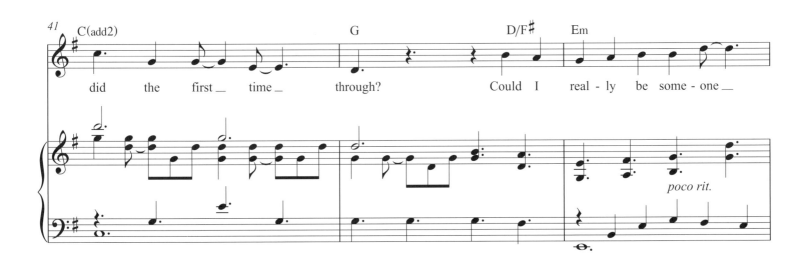

did the first___ time___ through? Could I real - ly be some - one___

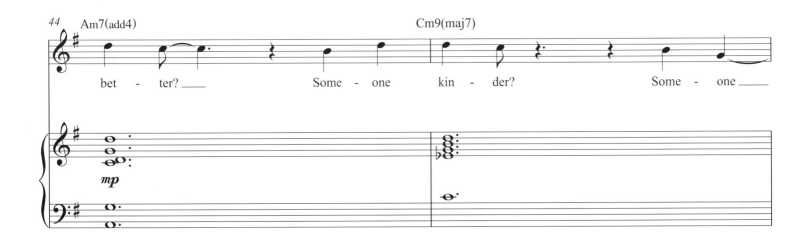

bet - ter? ___ Some - one kin - der? Some - one ____

BRINGIN' BACK CHRISTMAS

Music and Lyrics by
BENJ PASEK and JUSTIN PAUL

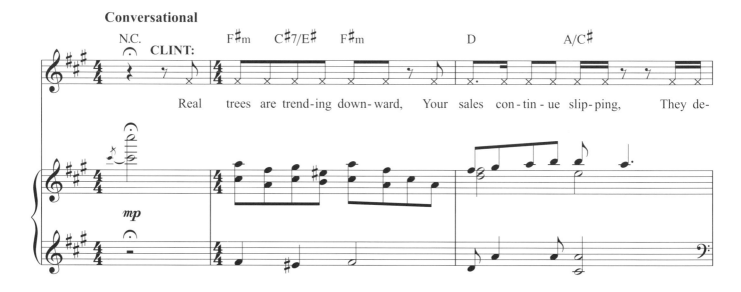

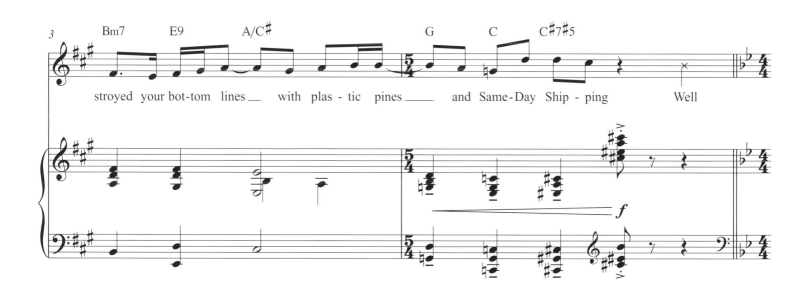

Copyright © 2022 Pick In A Pinch Music (ASCAP), Breathelike Music (ASCAP) and One Apple Park Songs (ASCAP)
All Rights for Pick In A Pinch Music and Breathelike Music Administered Worldwide by Kobalt Songs Music Publishing
All Rights for One Apple Park Songs Administered by Sony Music Publishing (US) LLC, 424 Church Street, Suite 1200, Nashville, TN 37219
All Rights Reserved   Used by Permission

Rat Pack Swing

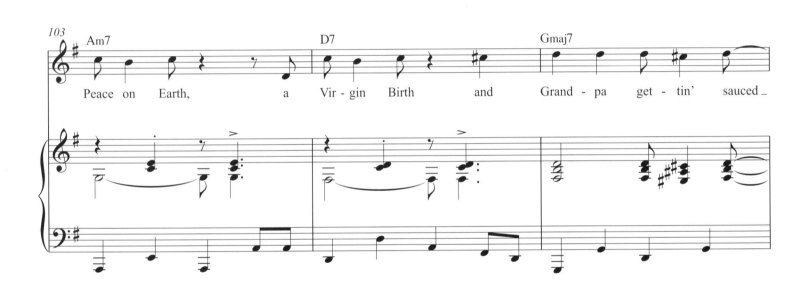

THE VIEW FROM HERE

Music and Lyrics by BENJ PASEK,
JUSTIN PAUL, KHIYON HURSEY,
SUKARI JONES and MARK SONNENBLICK

Expressive

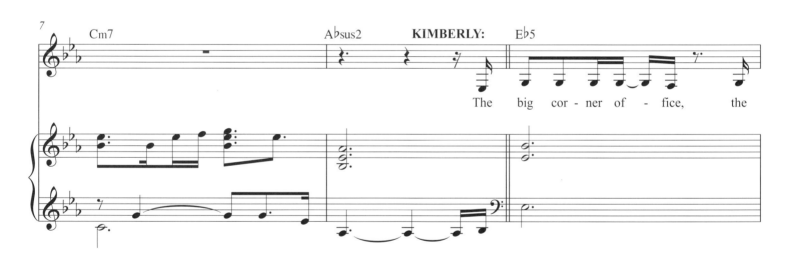

KIMBERLY: The big cor-ner of-fice, the

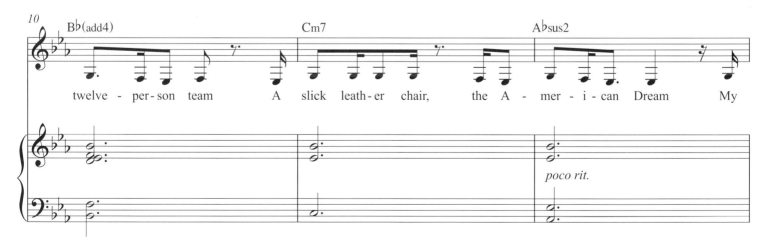

twelve-per-son team A slick leath-er chair, the A-mer-i-can Dream My

poco rit.

Copyright © 2022 Pick In A Pinch Music (ASCAP), Breathelike Music (ASCAP) and One Apple Park Songs (ASCAP)
All Rights for Pick In A Pinch Music and Breathelike Music Administered Worldwide by Kobalt Songs Music Publishing
All Rights for One Apple Park Songs Administered by Sony Music Publishing (US) LLC, 424 Church Street, Suite 1200, Nashville, TN 37219
All Rights Reserved   Used by Permission

THE STORY OF YOUR LIFE
(Marley's Haunt)

Music and Lyrics by BENJ PASEK,
JUSTIN PAUL, KHIYON HURSEY,
SUKARI JONES and MARK SONNENBLICK

Scary, with freedom

Menacing

MARLEY:

Ye shall find no sleep to-night, no
this is not a dream. Man-y wrongs have
ye to right Dark deeds ye must re-deem! _____

* Sounds where written

Copyright © 2022 Pick In A Pinch Music (ASCAP), Breathelike Music (ASCAP) and One Apple Park Songs (ASCAP)
All Rights for Pick In A Pinch Music and Breathelike Music Administered Worldwide by Kobalt Songs Music Publishing
All Rights for One Apple Park Songs Administered by Sony Music Publishing (US) LLC, 424 Church Street, Suite 1200, Nashville, TN 37219
All Rights Reserved Used by Permission

* Sounds an octave lower

44

CLINT BRIGGS: *I'm so sorry. I'm stuck on the first thing there. You said Past, Present, Future? Like A Christmas Carol? The Dickens story? The Bill Murray movie with Bobcat Goldthwait—*
MARLEY: *Yes, yes! Like the Dickens book and the Bill Murray movie and every other adaptation nobody asked for. Now, please, if you will just let me get this out. Sit.*

GOOD AFTERNOON

Music and Lyrics by BENJ PASEK ,
JUSTIN PAUL, KHIYON HURSEY,
SUKARI JONES and MARK SONNENBLICK

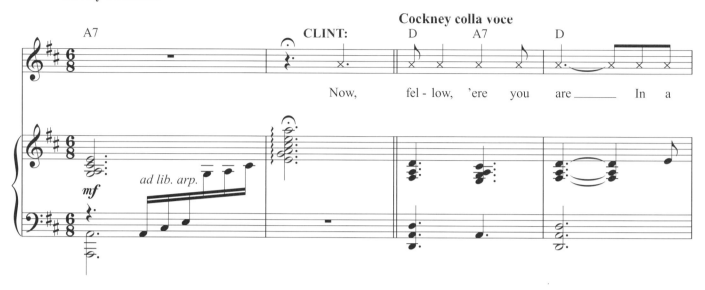

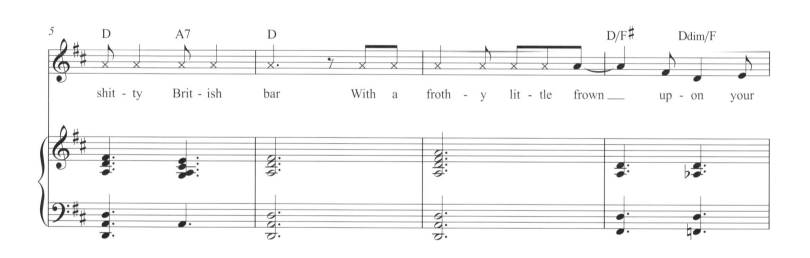

Copyright © 2022 Pick In A Pinch Music (ASCAP), Breathelike Music (ASCAP) and One Apple Park Songs (ASCAP)
All Rights for Pick In A Pinch Music and Breathelike Music Administered Worldwide by Kobalt Songs Music Publishing
All Rights for One Apple Park Songs Administered by Sony Music Publishing (US) LLC, 424 Church Street, Suite 1200, Nashville, TN 37219
All Rights Reserved   Used by Permission

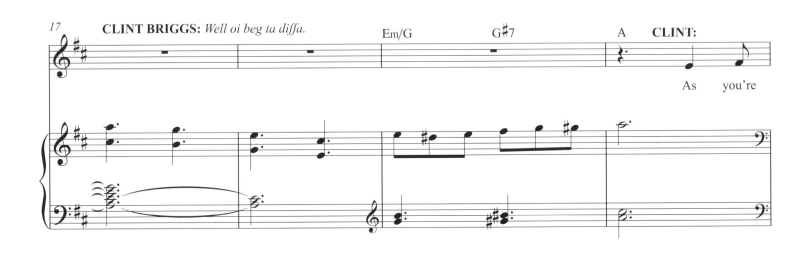

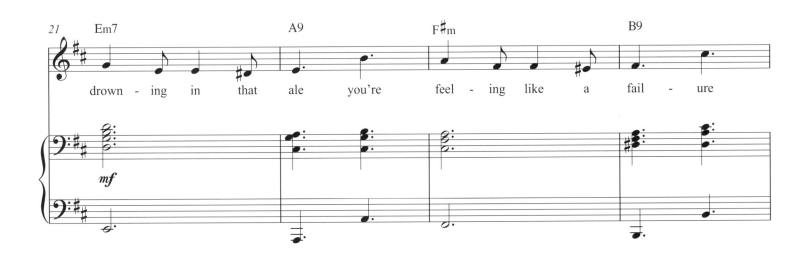

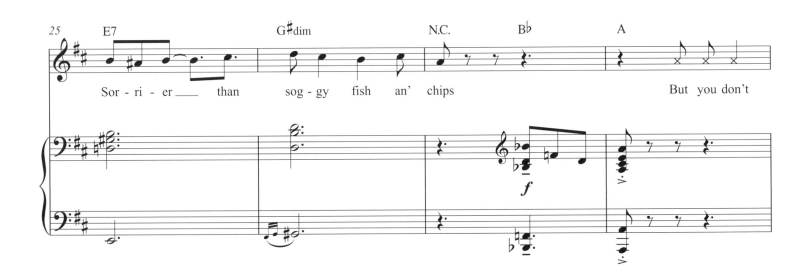

THE STORY OF YOUR LIFE
(Clint's Pitch)

Music and Lyrics by BENJ PASEK,
JUSTIN PAUL, KHIYON HURSEY,
SUKARI JONES and MARK SONNENBLICK

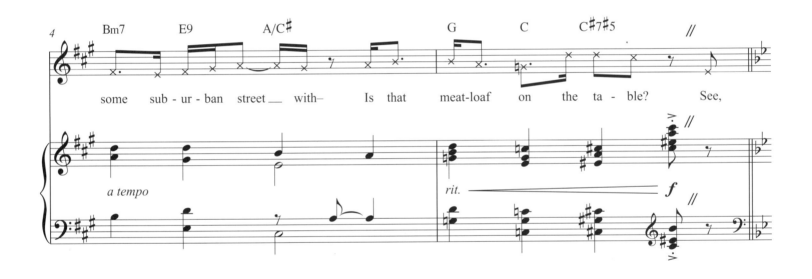

Copyright © 2022 Pick In A Pinch Music (ASCAP), Breathelike Music (ASCAP) and One Apple Park Songs (ASCAP)
All Rights for Pick In A Pinch Music and Breathelike Music Administered Worldwide by Kobalt Songs Music Publishing
All Rights for One Apple Park Songs Administered by Sony Music Publishing (US) LLC, 424 Church Street, Suite 1200, Nashville, TN 37219
All Rights Reserved   Used by Permission

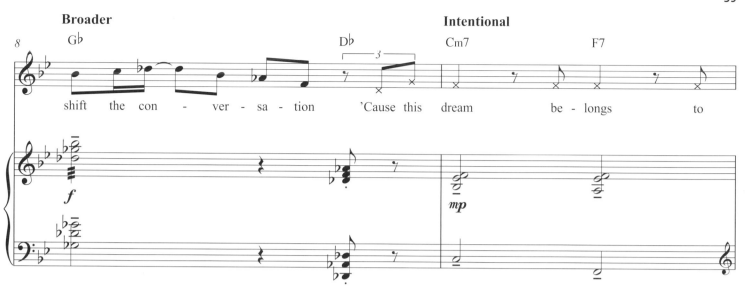

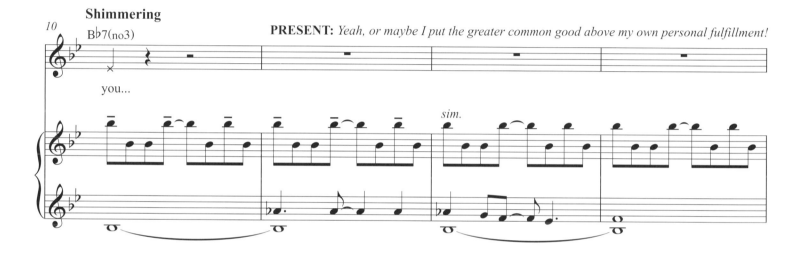

UNREDEEMABLE

Music and Lyrics by
BENJ PASEK and JUSTIN PAUL

Colla voce

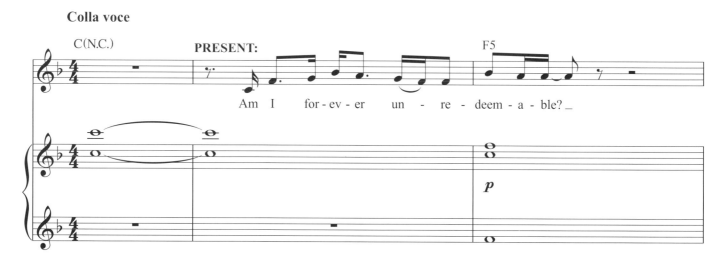

Am I for-ev-er un-re-deem-a-ble?

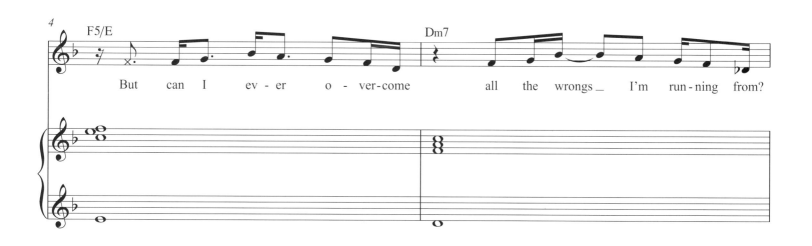

But can I ev-er o-ver-come all the wrongs I'm run-ning from?

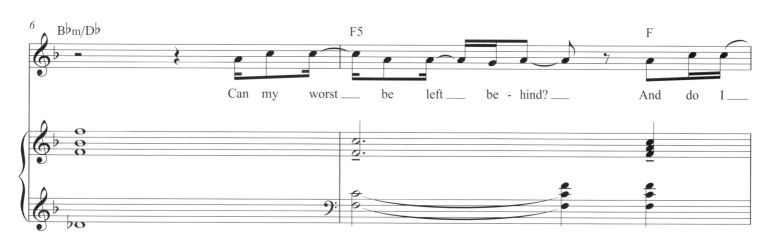

Can my worst be left be-hind? And do I

Copyright © 2022 Pick In A Pinch Music (ASCAP), Breathelike Music (ASCAP) and One Apple Park Songs (ASCAP)
All Rights for Pick In A Pinch Music and Breathelike Music Administered Worldwide by Kobalt Songs Music Publishing
All Rights for One Apple Park Songs Administered by Sony Music Publishing (US) LLC, 424 Church Street, Suite 1200, Nashville, TN 37219
All Rights Reserved   Used by Permission

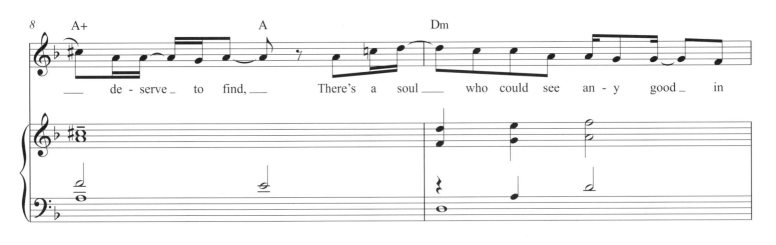

Moving forward

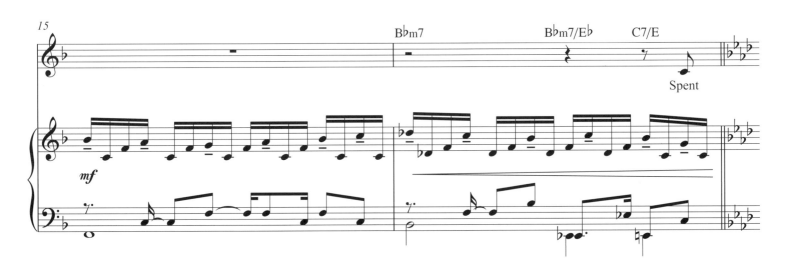

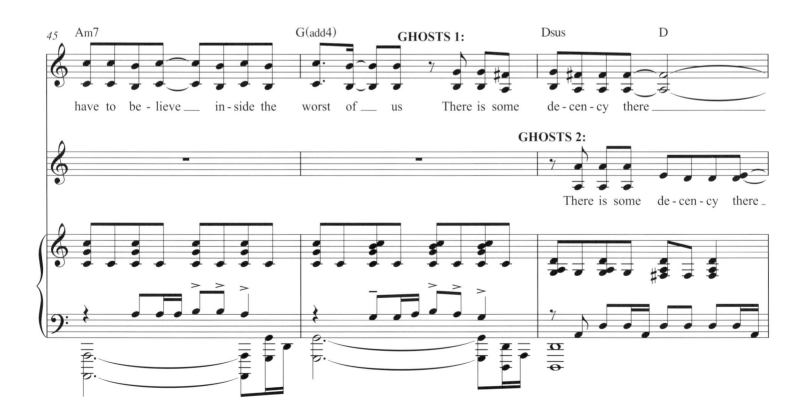

know _ if I _____ am for-ev-er un-re-

rall.

Sweeping

deem - a - ble _____ If I'll ev-er be _ some-one _

ALL GHOSTS:

Un - re - deem - a - ble ___ Ah

___ who makes up _ for all _ they've _ done Or is all _ I am un -

Ah _____

poco rit.

THE VIEW FROM HERE
(Riverwalk)

Music and Lyrics by BENJ PASEK,
JUSTIN PAUL, KHIYON HURSEY,
SUKARI JONES and MARK SONNENBLICK

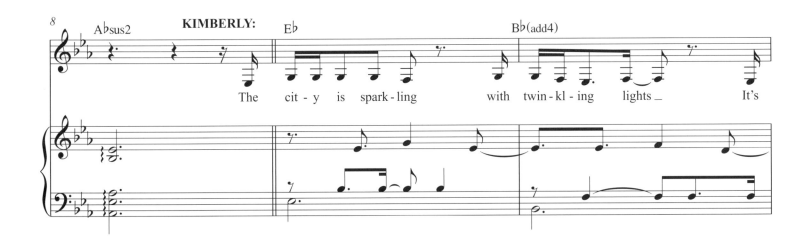

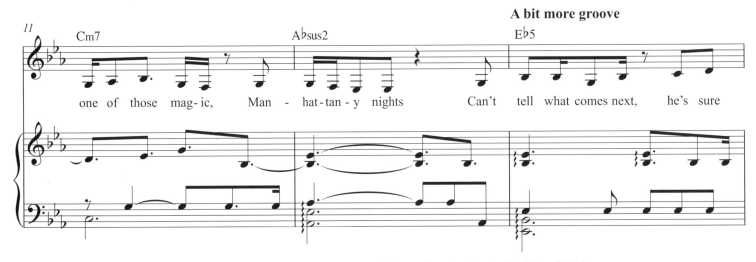

Copyright © 2022 Pick In A Pinch Music (ASCAP), Breathelike Music (ASCAP) and One Apple Park Songs (ASCAP)
All Rights for Pick In A Pinch Music and Breathelike Music Administered Worldwide by Kobalt Songs Music Publishing
All Rights for One Apple Park Songs Administered by Sony Music Publishing (US) LLC, 424 Church Street, Suite 1200, Nashville, TN 37219
All Rights Reserved   Used by Permission

'cause a brand new be-gin - ning feels long o-ver-due That's the view _

_ from here

That's the view _

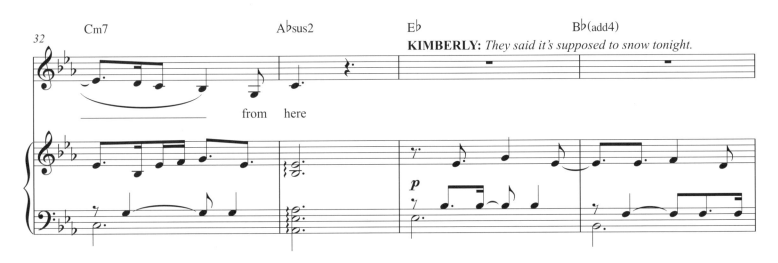

_ from here

KIMBERLY: *They said it's supposed to snow tonight.*

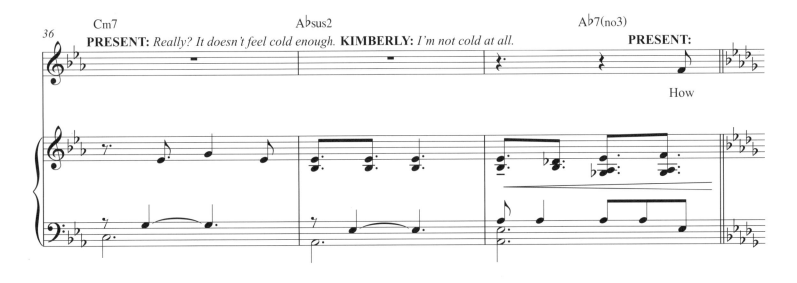

PRESENT: *Really? It doesn't feel cold enough.* **KIMBERLY:** *I'm not cold at all.*

PRESENT:

How

DO A LITTLE GOOD

Music and Lyrics by
BENJ PASEK and JUSTIN PAUL

Copyright © 2022 Pick In A Pinch Music (ASCAP), Breathelike Music (ASCAP) and One Apple Park Songs (ASCAP)
All Rights for Pick In A Pinch Music and Breathelike Music Administered Worldwide by Kobalt Songs Music Publishing
All Rights for One Apple Park Songs Administered by Sony Music Publishing (US) LLC, 424 Church Street, Suite 1200, Nashville, TN 37219
All Rights Reserved   Used by Permission

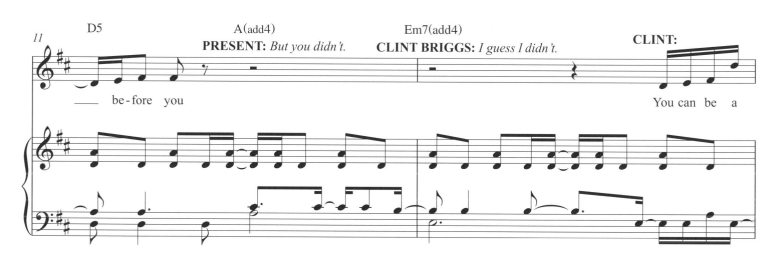

THAT CHRISTMAS MORNING FEELIN'
(Curtain Call)

Music and Lyrics by
BENJ PASEK and JUSTIN PAUL

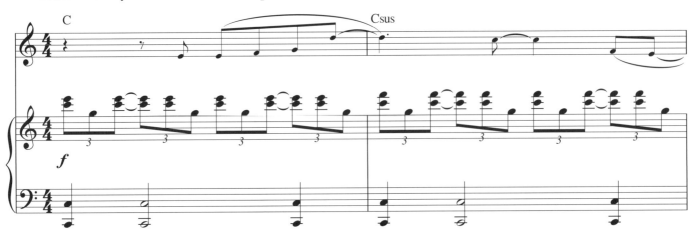

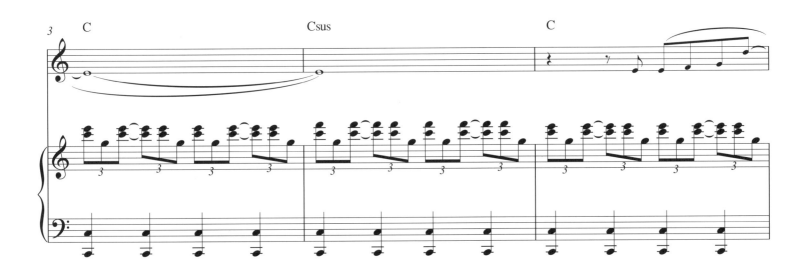

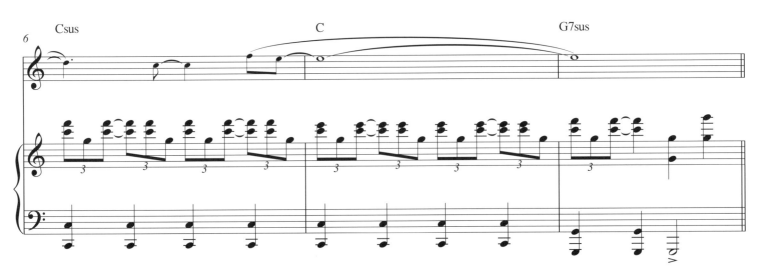

Copyright © 2022 Pick In A Pinch Music (ASCAP), Breathelike Music (ASCAP) and One Apple Park Songs (ASCAP)
All Rights for Pick In A Pinch Music and Breathelike Music Administered Worldwide by Kobalt Songs Music Publishing
All Rights for One Apple Park Songs Administered by Sony Music Publishing (US) LLC, 424 Church Street, Suite 1200, Nashville, TN 37219
All Rights Reserved   Used by Permission

Sounds where written.
**Sounds an octave lower.*

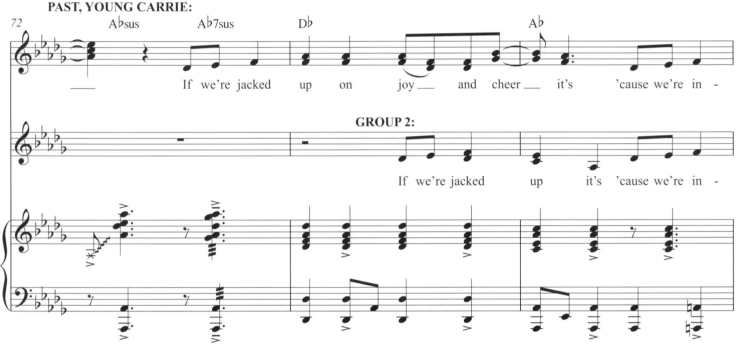

'Cause that's our af - ter - live - li - hood, __

GROUP 2:

Do - in' some good __

+ YOUNG CARRIE,
PAST, PRESENT, CLINT,
MARLEY, YET-TO-COME:

Play - in' our parts __ Chang - in' hearts __ One by

one __ And that Christ - mas morn - in' feel -

One by one by one And that Christ - mas morn - in' feel -

RIPPLE
(Cut Song)

Music and Lyrics by
BENJ PASEK and JUSTIN PAUL

Earnest anticipation

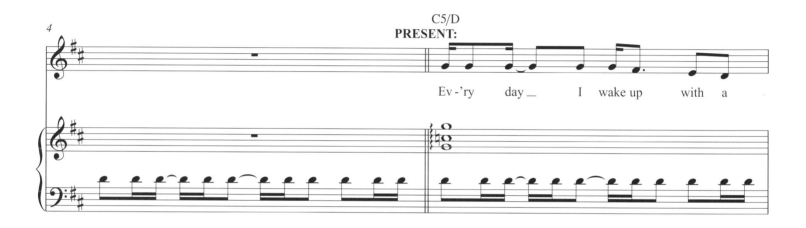

PRESENT:
Ev-'ry day __ I wake up with a

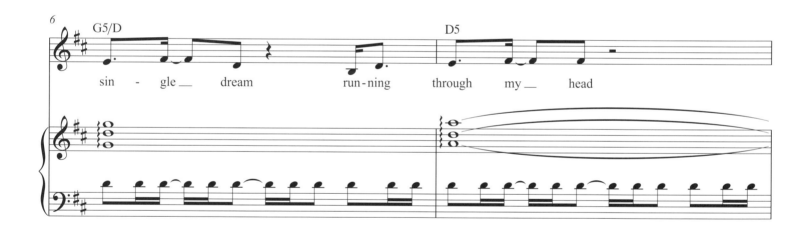

sin - gle __ dream run-ning through my __ head

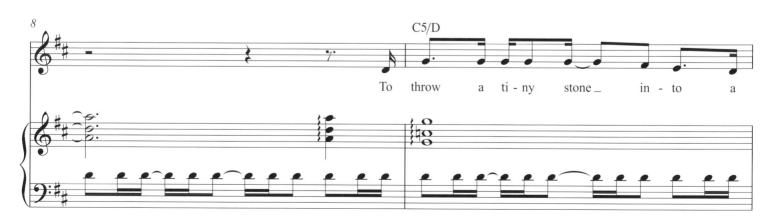

To throw a ti - ny stone __ in - to a

Copyright © 2022 Pick In A Pinch Music (ASCAP), Breathelike Music (ASCAP) and One Apple Park Songs (ASCAP)
All Rights for Pick In A Pinch Music and Breathelike Music Administered Worldwide by Kobalt Songs Music Publishing
All Rights for One Apple Park Songs Administered by Sony Music Publishing (US) LLC, 424 Church Street, Suite 1200, Nashville, TN 37219
All Rights Reserved   Used by Permission

might - y ___ stream and watch the rip - ples ___ as ___ they spread,

Well, we fall in line, fol - low

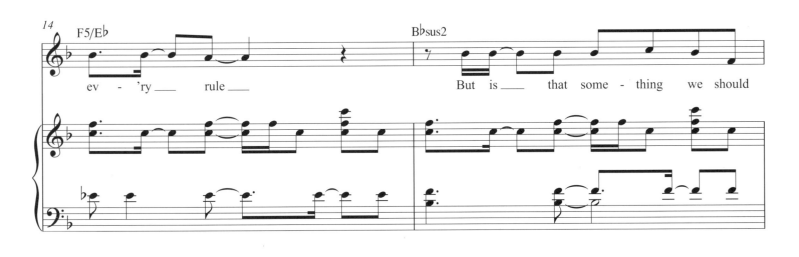

ev - 'ry ___ rule ___ But is ___ that some - thing we should

real - ly take pride in? 'Cause we're tread - ing wa - ter in the

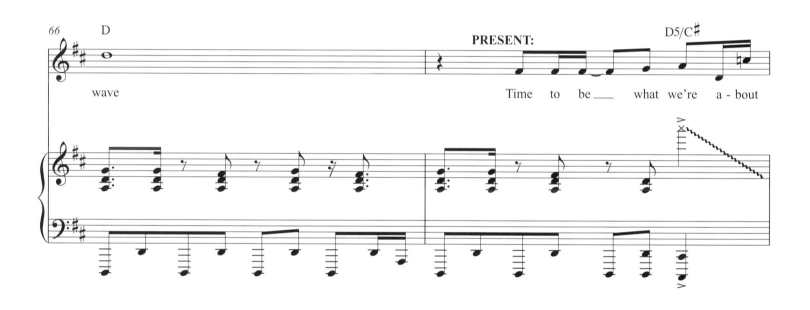

70
D
D5/C♯
brave
We need more than just a
Be - in' brave a
It's just called be - in' brave
72
Bm
G
rip - ple!
Make the choice to take a chance
rip - ple!
Ah
74
D
A5
PRESENT & GHOSTS:
Let's put on our big boy pants
If we on - ly skim the

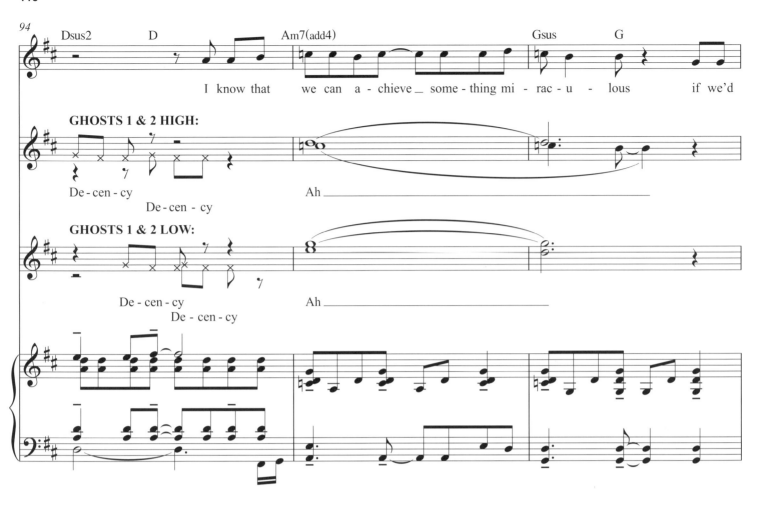

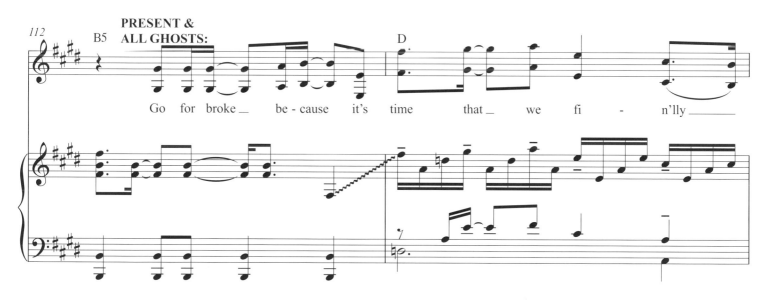

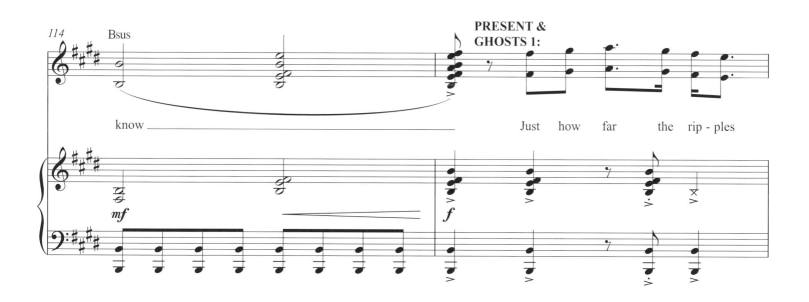